A Feast of Irish Cooking

A Feast of Irish Cooking

MOLLY O'NEILL

THE DOLMEN PRESS

Set in Palatino type by the Word Factory
and produced by Keats European Production Limited
for the publishers,

The Dolmen Press Limited
Mountrath, Portlaoise, Ireland

Designed by Liam Miller

First published 1986

ISBN 0 85105 4501

© 1986 Holly O'Neill

Contents

Appetizers

Cod's Roe Pâté

INGREDIENTS:

12 oz smoked cod's roe
  (in the piece)
1 tsp onion juice
¼ pt olive oil
1 cup fresh white
  breadcrumbs
8 oz cream cheese
tomato juice to taste
pepper

To garnish:
hot toast
unsalted butter
black olives
lemon quarters

DIRECTIONS:

Scrape the roe from the skin and put in a bowl with the onion juice. Pour the oil over the breadcrumbs and leave to soak for five minutes. Pound or beat the cod's roe with cream cheese until quite smooth, then work in the breadcrumbs and oil, a little at a time. Finish with tomato juice to taste and season with pepper. The mixture should be light and creamy. Pile into a shallow dish and serve with hot toast, unsalted butter, black olives and quarters of lemon.

Smoked Salmon Wheels

INGREDIENTS:

1 small brown loaf
4 oz butter
½ lb smoked salmon

juice of ½ lemon
ground black pepper
   (ground from mill)

DIRECTIONS:

Cut the crust lengthways from the top of the loaf, butter and cut thin slices from the length of the loaf. Cover each slice with smoked salmon and season with lemon juice and pepper. Trim away crust and roll each slice the length of the loaf like a swiss roll. Then cut each roll in thin slices.

Stuffed Tomato

INGREDIENTS:

8 tomatoes
salt and pepper
4 oz cream cheese

small bunch fresh chives
2–3 tblsps double cream
watercress to garnish

DIRECTIONS:

Skin the tomatoes. Cut a slice from the top (not the stalk end) of each tomato, reserve slices, hold tomato in hollow of your palm, flick out seeds with the handle of a teaspoon, using the bowl of the spoon to remove the core. Drain the hollowed-out tomatoes and lightly season inside each one with salt. Sieve the cheese by pushing it through a strainer. Season well and add some of the chives. Soften with cream. Fill the tomatoes with this cheese mixture with a teaspoon, replace their top slices on the slant and arrange them in a serving dish.

Stuffed Eggs

INGREDIENTS:

6 eggs
6 oz smoked cod's roe
2 oz unsalted butter
squeeze of lemon juice

1 oz gelatine
8 tblsps tomato juice
½ pt mayonnaise

For French dressing:
4 tblsps salad oil
salt
ground black pepper
juice and rind of ½ lemon

For tomato salad:
1 lb tomatoes
½ tsp caster sugar

DIRECTIONS:

Remove skin from cod's roe. Work butter in a bowl until soft with a wooden spoon. Cut eggs in half lengthways, remove yolks and push through a wire strainer. Pound the roe, butter and egg yolks together, adding lemon juice and 1–2 tablespoons of mayonnaise to make a creamy consistency. Fill egg whites, reshape each egg and arrange on a large plate. Scald and skin tomatoes, cut in thick slices and dust with sugar. Soak the gelatine in the tomato juice, dissolve over gentle heat and add to the mayonnaise. When the mayonnaise begins to thicken coat the eggs, using a large tablespoon, and let mayonnaise run on a serving dish. Mix together a dressing of oil, seasonings and lemon juice and pour on to tomatoes, place these around eggs on serving dish. Cut the lemon rind in fine shreds and cook in boiling water for one minute. Drain, dry on absorbent paper and scatter over the tomato salad.

Lobster Pancakes

INGREDIENTS:

1 lb lobster meat
½ pt white wine
1 oz butter
a few peppercorns
1 finely chopped onion

1 oz flour
finely chopped parsley
2 oz grated cheese
2–3 tblsps cream

DIRECTIONS:

Make pancakes (see page 82) and keep hot. Layer pancakes and place a sheet of greaseproof paper between each one. Cover over completely with greaseproof paper and place in a warm oven. Cook the lobster in boiling salted water for 30 to 40 minutes. Remove flesh from shell after cooking. Put wine and peppercorns into a saucepan and reduce by half by boiling over a fast heat until half the wine has evaporated. Strain and reserve remaining wine. Melt butter and fry onions over a gentle heat for two minutes until transparent. Add the flour and cook for a further minute. Gradually add the wine, chopped parsley and fish, bring to the boil, then remove from heat. Add cheese and cream. Divide the filling evenly between the pancakes and roll them up.

Shrimp Rounds with Cheese Cream

INGREDIENTS:

4 oz shelled shrimps
12–14 rounds of bread
 (1–1½ inches in
 diameter)
salt
pinch of cayenne
 pepper
½ oz butter

For cheese cream:
½ oz butter
½ oz flour
¼ pt creamy milk
1½ oz grated cheese
salt and pepper
English mustard

DIRECTIONS:

Heat some oil or butter and fry the bread until golden-brown, drain and keep warm. Toss the shrimps over the heat with the seasoning and butter and when the mixture is thoroughly hot pile it up on the bread. Put these in a flame proof dish and keep warm while preparing the cheese cream. Proceed as if making a white sauce, finish by gradually beating in the grated cheese. Season lightly and add mustard to taste. Spoon this cheese cream over the prepared bread and brown well under the grill. Serve hot

Crubeens

INGREDIENTS:

1 crubeen per person	bay leaf
1 carrot	thyme
1 onion	parsley
a few peppercorns	salt

DIRECTIONS:

Put the crubeens in a pan with the carrot, onion, salt, peppercorns, bay leaf, thyme and parsley. Cover with cold water, bring to the boil and simmer for three hours.

Pickled Herrings

INGREDIENTS:

12 herring fillets
salt and pepper
¼ pt vinegar
¼ pt beer
1 onion, sliced
1 carrot, sliced

1 oz sugar
1 bay leaf
1 bunch parsley
6 cloves
1 sprig thyme
6 peppercorns

DIRECTIONS:

Lightly salt and pepper the fillets and roll up into a curl.
Make pickle out of the vinegar and all the other ingredients, boil together for a half an hour. Put the curled herrings in a deep pie-dish and pour the pickle over them. Cover with a lid or foil and bake in a moderate oven for a half an hour. This dish is served cold and should be kept for at least 24 hours before serving.

Sweetbreads in Pots

INGREDIENTS: (per person)

1 slice of toast   salt and pepper
1 sweetbread   1 tblsp cream

DIRECTIONS:

Take a small ovenproof ramekin dish for each person. Put
in it a slice of buttered toast, a sweetbread, salt and pepper
and a tablespoon of cream. Put it in a slow oven and allow
it to stay in till all cream is absorbed, then put in a few
drops more and leave it for another ten minutes. Serve
hot.

Melon and Cucumber Salad

INGREDIENTS:

1 honeydew melon
1 lb tomatoes
1 large cucumber
salt
1 tblsp chopped parsley
1 heaped tsp mint and
 chives

For dressing:
2 tblsps wine vinegar
salt and pepper
caster sugar
6 tblsps salad oil

DIRECTIONS:

Cut the melon in half, remove flesh and cut into cubes. Skin and quarter the tomatoes. Peel the cucumber, cut in small cubes. Sprinkle lightly with salt, cover with a plate and stand for 30 minutes, drain away any liquid and rinse cubes with cold water. To make the dressing; mix the vinegar, seasoning and sugar together, whisk in oil. Mix the fruit and vegetables together in a deep bowl, pour over the dressing, cover and chill for 2–3 hours.

Soups

Potato and Leek Soup

INGREDIENTS:

2 lb potatoes
4 medium size leeks
1 oz butter
yolks of two eggs

1 pt milk
1 pt water
salt and pepper

DIRECTIONS:

Finely slice the white parts of the leeks, and sauté them in the butter. Peel and quarter the potatoes, and add them to the leeks. Add the milk and water and cook until the potatoes are soft. Pass the vegetables through a sieve. Lightly beat the yolks of the eggs, add them to the soup and allow to thicken, but take great care not to let the soup boil, otherwise it will curdle. Additional potatoes make the soup thicker, the eggs make it richer.

Farmhouse Vegetable Soup

INGREDIENTS:

4 carrots
1 small turnip
2 parsnips
2 onions
2 oz butter
1 clove garlic
15 fl oz stock

4 fl oz cream
salt
black peppercorns
bay leaf
parsley stalks
lemon thyme sprigs

DIRECTIONS:

Peel and slice vegetables. Melt the butter in a frying pan and add the sliced vegetables and cook gently for four minutes. Add soup stock. Add herbs and simmer for 20 minutes until vegetables are tender. Remove herbs. Place liquid and vegetables into a blender or pass through a sieve. Season to taste. Add cream and serve.

Pea and Ham Soup

INGREDIENTS:

cooked ham-bone and the
    remains of its meat
1 lb split green peas,
    soaked overnight
1 onion, stuck with two or
    three cloves

1 heaped tsp sugar
2 potatoes
3 pts water
salt and pepper

DIRECTIONS:

Put all the ingredients in a large pan and let them simmer until the peas are tender for about 1–1½ hours. Remove the ham-bone and pass the soup through a fine sieve. Add any shredded meat that remains before serving. Taste for seasoning.

Onion Soup

INGREDIENTS:

2 oz butter
1½ lb finely chopped onion
1 level tblsp flour
1 tsp salt and pepper
  combined
2 pts stock

To serve:
Thick slices of French
bread, one for each serving
  of soup.
Grated cheese

DIRECTIONS:

Melt fat in large pan, add onions, cook gently until soft.
Add flour and seasonings and cook for two minutes,
stirring. Stir in the stock, bring to boil and simmer for 30
minutes. Check for seasoning. Toast the slices of French
bread on one side only. Cover untoasted side of bread
thickly with cheese. Place under grill to melt. Place a slice
in each soup bowl, ladle soup over and serve at once.

Celery Soup

INGREDIENTS:

1 head celery
1 onion
1 white turnip
1 potato
2 pts white stock

½ pt milk
1 oz cornflour
1 oz flour
bouquet garni
salt and pepper

DIRECTIONS:

Prepare the vegetables and cut into slices. Place in saucepan with the stock and the seasonings and bring to the boil. Simmer until vegetables are soft. Rub through a sieve. Blend the flour and milk and bring to the boil. Add the soup and heat. Add cream when serving.

Tomato and Orange Soup

INGREDIENTS:

2 lb tomatoes
1 onion sliced
1 carrot sliced
1 strip of lemon rind
1 bay leaf
6 peppercorns
salt and pepper

2 pts stock
1 oz butter
3 tblsps flour
rind and juice of ½ orange
sugar to taste
¼ pt cream

DIRECTIONS:

Put tomatoes, onion and carrot into a pan with lemon rind, bay leaf, peppercorns and a good pinch of salt. Add stock to tomato mixture, put lid on and simmer for 30 minutes until tomatoes are pulpy, then rub through a sieve and set aside. Clean the pan, melt the butter in it, and stir in the flour. Pour on the tomato mixture, blend and bring to the boil. Shred the orange rind. Add the orange juice to soup, then seasoning and sugar to taste. Stir in the cream at the last moment and finally add the orange rind. Serve at once.

Lentil Soup

INGREDIENTS:

2 pts stock
4 oz lentils
1 onion
1 white turnip
1 oz flour
½ pt milk

1 oz butter
1 carrot
1 stick celery
salt and pepper
bouquet garni

DIRECTIONS:

Prepare the vegetables and cut into slices. Melt the butter and sauté the vegetables. Add the stock and bouquet garni. Bring to the boil, add lentils and boil until vegetables and lentils are soft.

Kidney Soup

INGREDIENTS:

½ lb beef kidney cubed
¼ lb round beef minced
1 carrot
1 onion
2 sticks celery
3 pts brown stock

1 oz flour
1 oz butter
bouquet garni
1 tblsp sherry
salt and pepper

DIRECTIONS:

Melt butter and brown vegetables slightly. Take up, add the flour, stock, minced beef and kidney. Add the bouquet garni, salt and pepper. Allow to simmer gently for about two hours. Take out a few pieces of kidney to act as a garnish and put remainder through a sieve. Bring to the boil again. Remove from heat and add sherry and kidney garnish.

Beef Tea

INGREDIENTS:

¼ lb lean beef   salt
¼ pt water

DIRECTIONS:

Remove any fat from the meat and shred finely. Put into an earthenware jar with water. Allow to stand for one hour. Cover the top with greaseproof paper and stand the jar in a saucepan of cold water. Bring slowly to the boil and then allow to simmer for one hour. Stir occasionally to prevent meat from sticking. Strain and leave to cool. Skim. Reheat when required and season with salt. Serve with dry fingers of toast or croutons.

Oxtail Soup

INGREDIENTS:

4 pts stock
2 carrots
1½ oz butter
bouquet garni

¼ oxtail
1 onion
1½ oz flour

DIRECTIONS:

Cut oxtail into sections. Remove any surplus fat. Wipe the sections with a damp cloth and dust a little of the flour over them. Prepare vegetables and fry in the butter. When browned remove and fry oxtail. Add vegetables, stock and bouquet garni. Bring to the boil. Simmer until the vegetables are soft and the oxtail thoroughly cooked (3–4 hours). Put vegetables through a sieve. Return to saucepan. Thicken if preferred.

Fish

Fish Pie

INGREDIENTS:

2 lb white fish (hake,
  haddock or cod)
2 whiting
4 oz peeled prawns
¼ lb mushrooms
1 large leek
¼ lb butter
anchovy essence

a few peeled grapes
1 tblsp cream
2 oz plain flour
¾ pt milk
1½ lb potatoes
salt, pepper, paprika and
  fennel

DIRECTIONS:

Put the whiting in a pint of water, bring to the boil, and simmer gently for 40 minutes, breaking the fish up with a fork during cooking. Strain liquid into another pan, and reduce until you have a half cup of concentrated stock. Poach the white fish in milk until tender. Make a roux with 2 oz flour and 2 oz butter, and gently add the milk in which the fish has cooked, until of a consistency which coats the back of the spoon. Add the fish concentrate, a little anchovy essence, a few grains of fennel seed, salt, pepper and a good teaspoon of paprika. Finely slice the leek and mushrooms and cook gently in butter. Peel and boil potatoes. Mix the cooked white fish with prawns, leek and mushrooms, the peeled grapes, the sauce enriched with a tablespoon of cream. Place all in a fireproof pie dish. Mash potatoes with milk and butter, season with salt and pepper. Cover the pie dish, dot with small pieces of butter, and cook in a moderate oven for 30 minutes or until the top is nicely browned.

Cod with Parsley Sauce

The cod, either in steaks or fillets, or even as a whole fish should be gently poached in a court bouillon: water to cover, about ½ cup of vinegar, a few black peppercorns, ½ teaspoon of fennel seeds. Cook until tender, lift out and drain carefully. With a sharp knife remove the skin. Decorate with a sprinkling of capers and chopped parsley and serve with boiled potatoes.

For Parsley sauce:

1 pt milk	1 bay leaf
1½ oz butter	salt and pepper
1½ oz flour	large handful parsley
½ onion, finely sliced	

DIRECTIONS:

Gently simmer the onion and bay leaf in the milk for 10 minutes. Make a roux with the flour and butter, and add the strained milk by degrees, until you have a smooth sauce. Boil for 5 minutes and taste for seasoning with salt and pepper. Chop the parsley very finely. Add by degrees to the white sauce and incorporate a nut of butter.

Mussel Chowder

INGREDIENTS:

1 lb mussels shelled
4 oz green streaky bacon
1 large chopped onion
1 stick of chopped celery
1 chopped green pepper
2 medium-size diced
  potatoes

1 bay leaf
¾ pt water
salt and pepper
1¼ oz flour
1 pt milk
1 oz chopped parsley

DIRECTIONS:

Remove the rind and cut bacon into dice; sizzle gently in a dry pan until turning colour, then add the onion and celery and cook until golden-brown. Add the green pepper, potatoes, bay leaf and water and bring to the boil. Season, and simmer until potatoes are tender, then draw pan aside. Blend the flour with ½ cup of the milk and add to the chowder; stir until boiling. Heat the rest of the milk and add to the chowder with the mussels. Simmer for 4–5 minutes before turning into a soup tureen. Scatter parsley over the top.

Stuffed Sea Trout

INGREDIENTS:

3 lb sea trout, cleaned and boned, with head removed

3 fl oz dry white wine

Fennel and Almond Stuffing:
1 oz butter
½ small onion, skinned and finely chopped
1 small fennel, finely chopped
1 garlic clove, crushed

2 oz fresh wholemeal breadcrumbs
2 oz toasted almonds, chopped
grated rind and juice of ½ lemon
pepper to taste

DIRECTIONS:

Make the stuffing. Melt the butter in a pan. Cook the onion, fennel and garlic for about 5 minutes, until soft. Stir in the breadcrumbs, almonds, lemon rind and juice and season. Open out the fish and spread the stuffing along one side. Fold over and put on a lightly greased piece of foil large enough to enclose the fish. Pour the wine over and seal the foil edges together. Carefully transfer to a roasting pan. Cook for 35–40 minutes until the fish is cooked through and the skin flakes easily when tested with a fork. Open out the foil and transfer the fish to a serving dish, then pour over any cooking juices and serve.

Haddock Kedgeree

INGREDIENTS:

1 small onion, skinned and chopped
1½ oz butter
1½ tsp medium curry powder
6 oz brown rice
1 pt fish stock or water
8 oz smoked haddock

1 egg, hard-boiled and chopped
2 tblsps chopped fresh parsley
salt and pepper to taste
finely grated rind of ½ lemon

DIRECTIONS:

In a large saucepan cook the onion in 1 oz of the butter for 3 minutes. Add the curry powder and cook for 1 minute further. Add the rice with the stock. Cover and simmer gently for about 30 minutes, until the rice is just tender and the liquid absorbed. Meanwhile, place the haddock in a large frying pan with just enough water to cover. Simmer for 10–15 minutes until tender. Drain, flake and discard all the bones. When the rice is cooked add the fish, egg, remaining butter, half the parsley and seasoning. Stir gently until heated through. Spoon into a warmed serving dish and sprinkle with the remaining chopped parsley and the grated lemon rind. Serve immediately.

Bradán Fillte
(Wrapped Salmon)

INGREDIENTS:

12 oz puff pastry
egg to glaze

sprigs of watercress
½ pint hollandaise sauce

For filling:
1 lb fresh salmon poached
salt and pepper
lemon juice
¼ lb mushrooms

6 spring onions
2–3 oz butter
2 hard-boiled eggs
6 oz long grain rice boiled

DIRECTIONS:

Remove the skin and bones from poached salmon and flake into a bowl, season with salt, pepper and lemon juice. Wash the mushrooms, dry and slice them. Trim and chop the spring onions and put in a pan with half the butter, cook them slowly for 1 minute then add the mushrooms and simmer for 5 minutes. Melt the remaining butter. Chop the eggs and add to the salmon with the rice, mushroom mixture and remaining melted butter. Taste for seasoning. Roll out puff pastry into a rectangle, cut of a 1-inch wide strip for decoration. Divide the remaining pastry into two (one piece ⅔ larger than the other). Put the salmon mixture on the larger piece and fold the pastry around it. Lay the other piece of pastry over the top, brush with egg and decorate. Bake for about 25–30 minutes. Garnish with watercress and serve with hollandaise sauce.

Sole with Orange

INGREDIENTS:

8 sole fillets, about 4 oz
 each, skinned
1 oz melted butter

orange segments,
 wholemeal bread,
 croutons and parsley
 sprigs, to garnish

For Orange Marinade:
finely grated rind of
 1 orange
juice of 2 oranges
1 small onion, finely
 chopped

2 tblsps chopped fresh
 parsley
salt and pepper, to taste

DIRECTIONS:

Mix together the marinade ingredients. Put the sole in a single layer in a shallow dish with the marinade. Cover and chill for at least 3 hours. Remove the sole from the marinade, place on a baking sheet and brush with the butter. Grill for 3–4 minutes, until the fish flakes easily. Place on a serving dish and keep warm. Put the marinade in a saucepan and bring to the boil. Cook for 3–4 minutes, until reduced and syrupy. Spoon over the fish. Garnish and serve at once.

Mackerel with Apple Sauce

1½ oz fresh wholemeal
  breadcrumbs
2 oz red eating apples,
  cored and chopped
1 oz walnut halves,
  chopped
grated rind of 1 lemon

1 tblsp chopped parsley
pepper to taste
6 fl oz medium sweet cider
4 mackerel, each 12 oz
  gutted, skinned and
  boned
4 tsp fresh thyme

For Apple Sauce:
12 oz cooking apples,
  peeled cored and sliced
juice of 1 lemon

1 oz sugar
½ tsp ground cloves

Mix together the breadcrumbs, apple, walnuts, lemon rind, parsley and pepper. Moisten with about 2 tablespoons of cider. Make 3 diagonal incisions across both sides of the fish. Sprinkle the thyme inside the fish then fill with the prepared stuffing, gently shaping the fish back together. Place the fish in an ovenproof dish large enough to hold them in a single layer and pour over the remaining cider. Cover and cook for 25–30 minutes or until cooked through and fish flakes easily when tested with a fork. Meanwhile, make the sauce. Put the apples, lemon juice, sugar and cloves into a small saucepan, cover and cook over a moderate heat for 10 minutes or until the apple is soft. Remove from the heat, allow to cool slightly, then purée in a blender or food processor. Arrange the cooked mackerel on individual warmed serving plates and serve with the warm apple sauce.

Smoked Cod and Onion Bake

INGREDIENTS:

2 lb smoked cod
1 lb small onions
½ pt milk
1 tblsp water

1 tsp cornflour
1 cup grated cheese
½ cup breadcrumbs
salt and pepper

DIRECTIONS:

Place smoked cod, onions and seasoning in a saucepan. Add milk and water. Bring to simmering point and gently simmer for 15 minutes. Carefully remove smoked cod and onions and place in a shallow ovenproof dish. Thicken sauce with cornflour and add to the dish. Sprinkle with grated cheese and breadcrumbs. Bake in the oven until golden.

Oven Baked Plaice

INGREDIENTS:

2 filleted plaice
1 raw potato
2 oz butter (for frying)
1 handful breadcrumbs
1 wineglass white wine
1 wineglass water
salt

6 peppercorns
bay leaf
blade of mace
½ oz butter
2 shallots, chopped
4 oz mushrooms, chopped
1 oz chopped parsley

For sauce:
1 oz butter
¾ oz flour

5 fl oz cream

DIRECTIONS:

Grate the potato on the coarse side of the grater. Soak it in cold water for half an hour, drain and dry well and separate the flakes with a fork. Fry in butter until crisp, then remove potato and fry the crumbs in the same way, keep them both warm. Skin the fillets, wash, dry and fold them. Lay in a buttered ovenproof dish, pour over the wine and water, add seasoning, bay leaf and mace. Poach for 10 minutes. Melt ½ oz butter in a pan, add shallots and after a few minutes, the mushrooms. Cook for 3–4 minutes, season well and add parsley. Pour off liquor from the fish. Make roux with the 1 oz butter and flour, add the liquor, stir until thickening, then add cream. Boil and then simmer for a few minutes. Arrange the mushroom mixture on the bottom of a serving dish. Place the fillets on top, coat with the sauce and scatter over the fried crumbs and potato.

Meat and Poultry

Steak and Guinness Stew

INGREDIENTS:

1½ lb round steak
6 oz mushrooms
2 onions
1 pt water
bouquet garni

salt and pepper
1 tsp vinegar
1½ oz flour
1½ oz butter
½ pt Guinness

DIRECTIONS:

Cut meat into large squares. Cut mushrooms into quarters. Slice onions. Sauté the meat in butter. Remove the meat from the pan and sauté the onions and mushrooms. Add the flour and slowly add the Guinness and water. Bring to the boil for 1 minute. Add the vinegar, bouquet garni, salt and pepper. Put all the ingredients into a casserole dish and cook for 1½–2 hours.

Stewed Tripe and Onions

INGREDIENTS:

1 lb tripe
2 onions
2 cloves
1 oz butter
1 oz flour

¾ pt milk
salt and pepper
sippets of toast and
   parsley to garnish

DIRECTIONS:

Put tripe into 1 inch squares. Put into cold water and bring to the boil. Boil for 1 minute. Pour off water and rinse tripe. Put back into saucepan with milk, whole onions, cloves and butter. Add seasonings. Stew gently for 1 hour. Add flour blended with the butter and cook for another five minutes. Season. Serve garnished with sippets of toast and parsley.

Rabbit Casserole

INGREDIENTS:

1 rabbit	¾ pt stock
1 lb streaky rashers	1 white turnip, sliced
1 oz flour	1 onion, sliced

DIRECTIONS:

Cut off legs of rabbit. Split it down the back. Cut into three pieces. Wash in warm water. Cut the rind off rashers. Fry in a hot pan. Lift out. Fry the sliced onion and rabbit and lift out. Add the flour. Stir over the heat until brown. Add the stock slowly. Boil for 4 minutes. Cool a little. Add the rabbit and sliced vegetables. Stew gently for two hours and serve.

Steak and Kidney Pie

INGREDIENTS:

6 oz rough puff pastry

1 lb steak
1 beef kidney
1 small onion
1 hard-boiled egg

eggs to glaze

a little stock
salt and pepper
1 tsp seasoned flour
parsley

DIRECTIONS:

Wipe steak and beat with the back of a wooden spoon. Cut into strips. Wash, skin and core the kidney. Put into small cubes. Coat the pieces of meat in seasoned flour. Place a piece of kidney on each strip of meat and roll up. Slice the onions and hard-boiled egg and place with the meat in a greased pie dish. Pour the stock over, add pepper and salt. Place a strip of pastry around the edge of the dish. Flake and flute the edges. Make a hole in the centre. Glaze with beaten egg. Place in a hot oven for the first 10 minutes and then reduce heat and cook for a further 1¼ hours.

Baked Liver and Bacon

INGREDIENTS:

½ lb lambs liver   4 rashers

For stuffing:
2 tblsps breadcrumbs   pinch mixed herbs
1 oz butter   salt and pepper
1 tsp parsley   stock to bind
½ tsp onion

DIRECTIONS:

Wash the liver in warm water and cut into ¼ inch slices. Rind and bone the rashers and cut in two. Make the stuffing and place about 1 desert spoon on each piece of liver in an ovenproof dish. Lay a slice of rasher on top of each. Pour a little water over and bake in a moderate oven for 20–30 minutes.

Stuffed Breast of Mutton

INGREDIENTS:

3 lbs of breast mutton
   boned
1 cup of breadcrumbs
1 small onion
1 tblsp parsley
¼ tsp dried herbs
salt and pepper
egg to moisten
oil to baste
½ pt boiling water

For stuffing:
Mix the crumbs, finely
chopped onion, parsley,
herbs, salt and pepper and
seasoning together.
Moisten with beaten egg.

DIRECTIONS:

Score the skin side – about 1½ inches apart to prevent it curling up. Lay uppermost on board the side from which the bones have been removed. Sprinkle lightly with pepper. Make a pocket in the meat and put in the stuffing. Roll up and tie with fine twine. Heat oil in a stew pan. Baste, and roast the mutton all over. Pour in boiling water and cover pan tightly. Cook for 25 minutes per pound and 25 minutes extra. Remove string. This dish is very good for cold cutting.

Irish Stew

INGREDIENTS:

2 lbs gigot chops
2 lb potatoes
4 onions
6 stalks celery

1 pt water
mixed herbs
salt and pepper
parsley to garnish

DIRECTIONS:

Wipe meat with a damp cloth. Peel potatoes and onions. Lay the meat on the bottom of a stewing pan and season. Cut the onion in rings and the celery in chunks and lay on top of the meat. Cut potatoes in two and lay on top. Pour over 1 pt water. Cover with the lid and stew gently for about 1½ hours. Garnish with parsley.

Spiced Beef

INGREDIENTS:

6 lbs brisket or silverside	1 lb salt
3 bay leaves	1 oz saltpetre
9–10 cloves	bunch of fresh mixed herbs
5 blades mace	3–4 sliced carrots
1 crushed clove garlic	3–4 sliced onions
2 oz brown sugar	

DIRECTIONS:

Wipe meat over with a damp cloth. Mix seasoning ingredients together except for carrots, onions and fresh herbs. Rub seasoning well into meat, then lay meat on bed of seasoning. Leave in a cool place. Repeat rubbing each day for 7 days. On the seventh day put the meat into a saucepan and cover with cold water. Bring to boiling point and simmer gently for 5 hours, when it should be tender. Put cooked meat on a flat dish and cover with a board. Set weight on top of board until meat is cold, when it is ready to carve and eat.

NOTE: The most important ingredient in a good spiced beef is time. If the spicing is hurried the meat will be tough and indigestible. But if the cooking is started at least a week in advance, the meat will be tender and melting.

Boiled Bacon and Cabbage

INGREDIENTS:

piece of boiling bacon   salt
cabbage   browned breadcrumbs

DIRECTIONS:

If very salty steep bacon overnight. Cook in tepid water and allow 25 minutes to the pound and 25 minutes extra. When cooked take up, peel off the skin. Dredge with breadcrumbs. Keep in a warm place.

For cabbage:
Trim cabbage and cut in quarters removing centre stalk. Wash the cabbage well in cold water. Drain well and cut into small pieces. Cook in the water in which the bacon has been boiled first bringing it to the boil.

Apricot Stuffed Lamb

INGREDIENTS:

4 lb leg of lamb, well
  trimmed and boned

Apricot and walnut stuffing:
2 oz ready-to-eat dried
  apricots, rinsed
1½ oz walnut halves,
  chopped

apricot halves and
watercress sprigs
  to garnish

2 oz fresh breadcrumbs
1 egg
1 tsp dried mixed herbs
salt and pepper to taste

DIRECTIONS:

To make the stuffing, chop the apricots and put in a bowl
with the walnuts, breadcrumbs, egg and herbs. Mix well
and season. Spoon the stuffing into the boned cavity in
the lamb, packing down. Using fine string and a trussing
needle, sew up the cavity. Place the joint on a meat rack in
a roasting pan and cover with foil. Cook for 1½ hours until
cooked through. Remove the foil 30 minutes before the
end of cooking time to brown meat. Stand in a warm place
for 10 minutes before carving, garnish and serve.

Honey Baked Ham

INGREDIENTS:

6 lb gammon
2 tblsps honey or brown
  sugar

pineapple rings and
  cherries or whole cloves

DIRECTIONS:

Soak ham in water for 24 hours to remove any excess salt.
Wrap ham in tin foil and place in a roasting tin and cook at
a moderate heat for 20 minutes per pound. Remove foil
and trim away fat. Cover ham with honey or brown sugar
and score surface diagonally. Trim with pineapple rings
with a cherry in the centre or stud with cloves. Put back in
oven and bake for half an hour until glazed.

Pork Fillets with Apples and Cider

INGREDIENTS:

3 pork fillets
2 tblsps oil
½ oz butter
1 small onion, chopped
1 eating apple, cored and
  sliced
1 wineglass cider

salt and pepper
5–10 tblsps stock
kneaded butter (2 parts
  butter to 1 part flour
  worked to a paste)
1 oz chopped parsley

DIRECTIONS:

Brown fillets all over in pan of oil and butter. Take out and add onion and apple. Fry for a few minutes, then add fillets, cider and a little stock. Season, cover and simmer for 25 minutes or until tender. Take up fillets, slice diagonally and keep hot. Strain gravy, return to pan and thicken lightly with a little kneaded butter. Adjust seasoning, add parsley and put in pork. Heat gently and serve.

Homemade Meat Roll

INGREDIENTS:

2 lb beef, minced
2 lb ham, minced
2 lb breadcrumbs
1 level tsp mixed spice

a little grated nutmeg
2 large eggs, slightly beaten
4 oz flour
4 oz toasted breadcrumbs

DIRECTIONS:

Mix the beef, ham, breadcrumbs, spices and nutmeg together. Bind with the slightly beaten eggs. Break the mixture into three 2 pound rolls. Liberally cover three boiled pudding cloths with the flour. Stitch the meat rolls into these pudding cloths. Drop the rolls into a large pan of boiling water and simmer gently for 4 hours. Then lift out the rolls from the pan, remove from the pudding cloths. Roll in the toasted breadcrumbs. Allow to stand for at least a few hours in the bottom of the refrigerator before serving chilled.

Chicken with Spring Onion Stuffing

INGREDIENTS:

1 tblsp corn oil
2 celery sticks, trimmed and chopped
2 tsps ground coriander
1 leek, trimmed and chopped
6 spring onions, chopped
3 oz fresh breadcrumbs
1 egg yolk, beaten
3 lb oven-ready chicken
juice of ½ lemon
pepper to taste
spring onions and celery leaves, to garnish

DIRECTIONS:

Heat the oil in a large frying pan and add the celery. Cover and cook gently for 2–3 minutes, until soft. Add the coriander and remaining vegetables and cook gently, stirring occasionally, for a further 2–3 minutes. Remove the pan from the heat and stir in the breadcrumbs and egg yolk. Press a little of the stuffing into the neck of the bird and secure the flap of the skin with a wooden cocktail stick. Put the remaining stuffing into the main cavity and tie the legs together. Place the chicken on a roasting rack in a roasting pan. Use the lemon juice to baste the bird and season with pepper. Bake for 1 hour or until the chicken is golden brown. Garnish with spring onions and celery leaves.

Hot Chicken with Avocado

INGREDIENTS:

4 boned, skinned chicken
  breasts
1 small egg for coating
salt and pepper

For avocado mousse:
1 large ripe avocado
juice of ½ lemon
1 oz chopped raw onion
1 crushed garlic clove
pinch of chilli powder

5 tblsps sesame seeds
1 oz butter
1 tblsp olive oil
4 lettuce leaves

1 tomato, skinned and
  chopped
½ tsp coriander seeds,
  crushed

DIRECTIONS:

First make the mousse. Pulp the avocado flesh in a blender with the other ingredients, season to taste. Place the mousse in small ramekins and freeze for about 1 hour until the outside is set and the inside thoroughly chilled. Turn the chicken breasts in the beaten egg and seasoned sesame seeds until well coated. Heat the oil and butter and fry the chicken both sides until brown and crisp on the outside and cooked through for about 15 minutes. Turn out each avocado mousse on to a lettuce leaf, use these to garnish the serving plate. Add the hot chicken breasts and serve immediately.

Roast Duck with Honey

INGREDIENTS:

1 large duck with giblets
1 tsp oil
salt
1 onion
½ oz butter

2 tblsps clear honey
juice of ½ lemon
1 tblsp arrowroot mixed
  with 2 tblsps water

For stuffing:

1 oz butter
1 medium-size chopped
  onion
4 oz chopped cashew nuts
4 oz fresh breadcrumbs
grated rind of 1 lemon
1 tblsp chopped parsley

1 tsp chopped sage
1 tsp chopped thyme
½ tsp cinnamon
salt and pepper
1 beaten egg
juice of ½ lemon

For garnish:

½ bunch of watercress

1 sliced lemon

DIRECTIONS:

Brown the giblets, but not the liver, in 1 teaspoon oil, cover with 1 pint cold water, bring to the boil and skim well. Season with salt and 1 onion washed and trimmed but not peeled and simmer gently for 30–45 minutes. Strain to make stock. To prepare stuffing, melt half the butter, add the onion and cook slowly until soft but not coloured, drop the remaining butter into the pan and when melted add the nuts and fry until golden brown. Turn the nuts and onions into a bowl, add the rest of the ingredients and mix well. Stuff into the body of the duck and truss neatly. Rub the ½ oz butter over the duck and then spread with the honey. Roast for 1½ hours (15 minutes per pound and 15 minutes over), basting and turning from time to time. Take up the duck, remove the trussing strings, trim the leg and wing joints and set on the serving dish. Tip off the fat, leaving any sediment at the bottom of the pan, add the strained lemon juice and stock. Bring to the boil, season well and thicken with the arrowroot. Garnish the duck with watercress and lemon slices, and serve with the gravy.

Vegetables

Colcannon

INGREDIENTS:

1½ lbs potatoes steamed
  and mashed
12 oz kale freshly cooked

8 oz onions trimmed and
  sliced
¼ pt creamy milk
2 oz butter

DIRECTIONS:

Melt a little butter in a pan and sauté the onion or leek for a few minutes until just tender. Combine the potatoes and kale, add onion, milk and butter and beat well. Season with salt and pepper.

Parsnip Fritters

INGREDIENTS:

3 medium-size parsnips
3 tblsps plain flour
1 tblsp olive oil
1 egg white

pinch of bicarbonate of
  soda
salt and pepper

DIRECTIONS:

Scrape the parsnips, halve and quarter them, cut the quarters into pieces 1 inch long. Boil in salted water until tender. Meanwhile, make the batter. Put the flour into a bowl with a pinch of salt. Add the oil, and mix. Now add warm water to make a batter like thick cream. When the parsnips are cooked, drain them, dry on paper towels, and season with salt. Beat an egg to a stiff froth, until it forms peaks. Add a pinch of bicarbonate of soda to the batter, and beat in a spoonful of the egg white. Now fold in the rest of the white, and drop the parsnip pieces in the batter, see that they are well coated. Deep fry in smoking hot oil, until they are well puffed up and golden. Dredge with salt, and serve.

Bubble and Squeak

INGREDIENTS:

8 oz cold mashed potatoes   2 oz butter
8 oz cooked cold cabbage   1 tsp vinegar
salt and pepper

DIRECTIONS:

Mix the potatoes and cabbage together and season well. Melt the butter in a large frying pan and add. Cook until potato and cabbage is thoroughly hot. Sprinkle the vinegar on top of the mixture and serve. Chopped left-over corned beef may be added to this mixture.

Stuffed Vegetable Marrow

INGREDIENTS:

1 medium-size marrow	1 oz butter
1 tsp sea salt	mixed herbs
1 cup cooked rice	salt and pepper
1 cup cold minced meat	tomato purée
1 finely chopped onion	1 tblsp stock

DIRECTIONS:

Peel the marrow and cut it into rings about 1½ inches deep. Remove the centre core of seeds and sprinkle with coarse salt. Leave for 15 minutes, and rinse. Arrange the pieces in a shallow baking dish and fill the cavities with a mixture of cooked rice, minced cold meat, a sprinkling of mixed herbs, salt and plenty of pepper. The stuffing may be pre-cooked, having sautéed a finely chopped onion in butter, adding the minced meat, herbs, seasoning and rice. Add also a teaspoon tomato purée and a little stock. Fill the cavities, dot with butter and bake in a moderate oven. Sprinkle with a mixture of chopped parsley and breadcrumbs and brown under the grill before serving.

Cheese-Topped Vegetables

INGREDIENTS:

1 small cauliflower, cut into florets

8 oz Brussels sprouts, trimmed

1 tblsp whole grain mustard

2 oz mature Cheddar cheese, grated

1 oz fresh breadcrumbs

DIRECTIONS:

Steam the cauliflower and sprouts until just tender. Mix together with the mustard in an ovenproof dish. Mix together the cheese and breadcrumbs, then sprinkle over the vegetables. Place under a hot grill and cook for about 2 minutes until the cheese is melted.

Leek and Tomato Bake

INGREDIENTS:

1½ lb leeks, trimmed and
    sliced
1 oz butter
1 oz plain flour
½ pt milk
1 tsp ground mace
½ tsp grated nutmeg
salt and pepper to taste
4 tomatoes, sliced

½ bunch watercress,
    trimmed and roughly
    chopped
2 oz mature Cheddar
    cheese, grated
tomato slices and
    watercress sprigs to
    garnish

DIRECTIONS:

Cook the leeks in boiling water for 8–10 minutes, or until tender, then drain. Melt the butter in a saucepan add the flour and cook over a low heat for 1 minute. Gradually add the milk, stirring constantly. Bring to the boil, add the mace, nutmeg and seasoning. Add the leeks and tomatoes and stir carefully. Transfer the mixture to a shallow ovenproof dish and smooth over the top. Sprinkle over the watercress and cheese and cook under a medium-hot grill for 5 minutes, until the cheese melts and is golden-brown. Serve hot, garnished with tomato slices and watercress sprigs.

Desserts

Carrageen Blanc-Mange

INGREDIENTS:

¾ oz carrageen
1 pt milk

sugar or honey, to taste
lemon rind

DIRECTIONS:

Add carrageen and lemon to milk and bring to the boil. Simmer gently for 15 minutes and stir. Strain. Add sugar or honey. Pour into a wet mould and leave until set. Turn out and decorate.

Carrot Pudding and Vanilla Sauce

INGREDIENTS:

2 oz flour
½ cup grated carrot
1 cup fresh breadcrumbs

2 oz chopped suet
2 oz sultanas

grated nutmeg
1 egg
1 tsp baking powder

1 cup milk
castor sugar to dress

Vanilla sauce:
½ oz sugar
½ oz flour
½ oz butter

1 cup milk
vanilla essence

DIRECTIONS:

Mix all the dry ingredients together. Add beaten egg and as much milk as will make a nice pudding consistency. Mix well together and put into a greased bowl. Cover with greaseproof paper and steam for two hours. Take up and turn out into a hot dish. Dredge the top with castor sugar.

Melt butter and flour, stir until blended. Add the milk gradually stirring all the time. Add sugar and boil for at least four minutes. Add about three drops of vanilla essence. Pour over carrot pudding and serve at once.

Rice Pudding

INGREDIENTS:

1 oz rice
½ pt milk
½ oz butter

½ oz sugar
1 egg
lemon rind

DIRECTIONS:

Wash the rice. Put into double saucepan with the milk and lemon rind. Cook for about 1 hour. Remove lemon rind. Add the sugar and the butter. Cool a little and add beaten egg. Pour into a greased pie dish and cook in a moderate oven until set and golden brown on top. Sprinkle with castor sugar and serve warm.

Stewed Apples and Custard

INGREDIENTS:

4 cooking apples
⅛ pt water

2 oz sugar
whole cloves

Custard:
1 large egg
½ pt milk

vanilla essence
grated nutmeg

DIRECTIONS:

Core apples and peel thinly. Cut into eighths. Make a syrup with the water and sugar. Add apples and cloves and stew very gently until soft. Lift out carefully onto a dish and make the custard.

Beat egg well in a bowl. Heat milk, sugar and essence together. Pour over the beaten egg, whisking it all the time. Put back in saucepan, and stir over gentle heat until custard coats the back of a wooden spoon. Serve the custard in a small jug and sprinkle with nutmeg.

Gooseberry Fool

INGREDIENTS:

1 lb gooseberries
2 tblsps water

sugar to sweeten
½ pt cream

DIRECTIONS:

Top and tail gooseberries. Wash and drain. Put into a greased saucepan. Add the water and cook until soft. Add enough sugar to sweeten. Rub through a fine sieve. Fold in whipped cream and serve in individual dishes.

Brown Bread Ice Cream

INGREDIENTS:

4 oz fresh wholemeal
  breadcrumbs, including
  crusts
3 oz light brown sugar

5 fl oz whipped cream
10 fl oz natural yoghurt
2 egg whites

DIRECTIONS:

Mix the breadcrumbs with 2 oz of the sugar and spread on a baking sheet. Bake in a moderate oven for 10–15 minutes, turning occasionally, until crisp and lightly browned. Set aside to cool, then break up. Whip the cream until thick, then stir in the yoghurt and remaining sugar. Stir in the toasted breadcrumbs, reserving 1 oz for the topping. Whisk the egg white and fold into mixture. Pour into a freezerproof container and freeze for 4 hours, until firm. Transfer to the refrigerator to soften 30 minutes before serving. To serve, scoop into serving dishes and sprinkle with the reserved crumbs.

Breads and Cakes

Brown Bread

INGREDIENTS:

12 oz plain flour
12 oz wheatmeal
1 tsp bread soda

1 tsp salt
¾ pt buttermilk

DIRECTIONS:

Combine the dry ingredients in a bowl. Make a well in the centre and add the buttermilk all at once. Mix with a fork to a soft dough. Transfer to a greased loaf tin. Bake in a hot oven for 45 minutes.

Soda Bread

INGREDIENTS:

1 lb flour
½ tsp bread soda

½ tsp salt
½ pt buttermilk

DIRECTIONS:

Sieve flour, bread soda and salt into a bowl. Make a well in the centre and add the buttermilk all at once. Mix to a nice loose dough. Put on to a floured board. Knead lightly with the fingers to remove all cracks. Flatten to about 2 inches in height. Make a cross on top with a knife dipped in buttermilk. Place on a greased tin and bake in a hot oven for about 45 minutes.

Tea Scones

INGREDIENTS:

½ lb flour
½ oz sugar
1½ oz butter
1 egg

1 tsp baking powder
1 fl oz milk
2 oz sultanas (optional)

DIRECTIONS:

Sieve flour and rub in the butter. Add sugar, baking powder and sultanas and mix well. Make a well in the centre and add the beaten egg and a little milk to make a loose dough. Put onto a floured board and knead slightly, flatten out to about 1 inch in height. Cut into rounds. Put onto a greased baking sheet and bake in a hot oven for about 15 minutes. If liked, tops may be brushed with beaten egg to glaze.

Potato Cakes

INGREDIENTS:

8 oz cooked potatoes
4 oz flour
½ oz butter

¼ tsp salt
¼ tsp baking powder
1 fl oz milk

DIRECTIONS:

Sieve flour, salt and baking powder into a bowl. Rub in the butter. Mash potatoes and add to the flour. Mix thoroughly and add milk. Put onto a floured board and knead. Roll out to ¼ inch thickness and cut into rounds. Grease griddle or frying pan until very hot and fry cakes to a golden brown on each side. Serve hot with butter.

Pancakes

INGREDIENTS:

2 oz flour
¼ pt milk
1 egg
salt

oil for frying
castor sugar
lemon

DIRECTIONS:

Sieve flour and salt into a bowl. Make a well in the centre and drop in the egg. Mix well. Add half the milk and beat to a smooth paste. Leave for about five minutes and add remainder of milk. Mix well and pour into a jug. Cover and leave aside for about one hour. (The pancake batter may now be used for savory fillings). Grease a small frying pan with oil, pour on a thin layer of pancake mixture. Fry to a golden brown. Toss and cook the other side. Dredge with castor sugar and sprinkle with lemon juice. Roll up and serve hot.

Barm Brack

INGREDIENTS:

1 lb flour
2 oz butter
2 oz sugar
¾ oz yeast

½ pt milk
1 egg
8 oz sultanas
2 oz mixed candied peel

To glaze:
Syrup of sugar and water

DIRECTIONS:

Warm the flour, rub in the butter, add sugar, yeast and beaten egg and enough warm milk to mix to a batter. Beat until smooth and elastic in texture. Fold in fruit and candied peel. Allow to rise in a greased tin until double its size. Brush with the syrup of sugar and water and bake in a very hot oven for 10 minutes lower the temperature to a moderate heat and continue to bake for a further 35 minutes.

Ginger Cake

INGREDIENTS:

¼ lb butter
¼ lb moist sugar
½ lb flour
1 tsp ground ginger
¼ tsp bread soda
¼ tsp cream of tartar

1 tsp parisian essence
2 eggs
4 oz preserved ginger
1 fl oz treacle
1 fl oz golden syrup

DIRECTIONS:

Line a six inch cake tin. Cream the butter, sugar and essence. Add treacle and golden syrup. Sieve flour, bread soda and cream of tartar into mixture. Drop in the eggs one at a time and beat. Add the flour and the preserved ginger cut up into cubes. Put mixture into prepared tin and bake in a moderate oven for 1¼ hours.

Guinness Cake

INGREDIENTS:

8 oz butter
8 oz brown sugar
½ pt Guinness
1½ lb mixed dried fruits
4 oz candied peel

1¼ lb plain flour
1 tsp bicarbonate of soda
1 tsp nutmeg
1 tsp mixed spice
3 eggs

DIRECTIONS:

Grease a nine inch cake tin and line with greaseproof paper. Put the butter, sugar and Guinness in a saucepan and bring to the boil slowly, stirring all the time until the sugar and butter have melted. Mix in the fruit and candied peel and bring the mixture back to the boil. Simmer for five minutes. Remove from heat and stand to go cold. Sift flour, spices and bicarbonate of soda into a large mixing bowl, stir in cold fruit mixture and beaten eggs, turn into cake tin and bake in a low oven for two hours. Cool in tin before turning out.

Christmas Fare

Turkey Broth

INGREDIENTS:

2 pts strong turkey stock
3 tblsps carrot finely diced
2 tblsps chopped onions
2 tblsps long grain rice

salt and pepper
3 tblsps cream
1 oz chopped parsley

DIRECTIONS:

Prepare stock from turkey giblets by adding enough water just to cover. For a strong, clear stock, simmer it gently, don't boil hard. Strain and leave to cool, remove all fat. Put the stock, vegetables and rice in a pan, season, cover and simmer for 30–40 minutes. Taste for seasoning. Stir in cream, sprinkle with chopped parsley and serve.

Roast Turkey with Oyster Stuffing

INGREDIENTS:

1 16 lb hen turkey
giblets
diced root vegetables

salt and pepper
arrowroot to thicken
2 oz butter softened

For oyster stuffing:
12 oz canned oysters
1 large chopped onion
6 oz butter
3 cups breadcrumbs

3 sticks of chopped celery
1 tsp mixed dried herbs
1 tblsp chopped parsley
little milk to bind

DIRECTIONS:

First prepare the stock for the gravy. Put the giblets, root vegetables and seasoning in a large pan with water to cover and simmer for 1–2 hours, strain and keep stock aside for the gravy. Thicken it with a little arrowroot, and colour it, if necessary, with a little of your favourite gravy browning.

To prepare oyster stuffing:
Cook the onion in butter until it is golden and add about ⅓ of the breadcrumbs and stir over heat until all the butter is absorbed. Tip mixture into a bowl, add the remaining crumbs, celery, herbs and seasoning. Drain, rinse and drain the oysters, lightly chop them, add to the mixture and bind with a little milk. Wipe out the cavity of the turkey with a damp cloth and rub the inside with ½ teaspoon salt. Put in the stuffing, sew up with fine string. Rub turkey with the softened butter and wrap in foil. Cook for 4–4½ hours, unwrapping the foil and increasing the heat for the last 20 minutes.

Roast Potatoes

Choose medium to large potatoes of even size. Peel and blanche by putting into cold salted water and bringing to the boil. Drain thoroughly and lightly scratch the surface with a fork. Put the potatoes into smoking hot fat in the same tin as the meat, 40–45 minutes before the meat is fully cooked, and baste well. Cook until soft, basting them when you baste the meat and turning after 25 minutes.

Brussels Sprouts

INGREDIENTS:

2 lb small sprouts
salt

1 oz butter
ground black pepper

DIRECTIONS:

Trim the sprouts, removing any loose outside leaves and wash well in cold salted water, drain. Cook uncovered in a large pan of boiling salted water until just tender, no longer than 8 minutes after the water has reboiled. Drain well and return to pan with a knob of butter, simmer for 2–3 minutes. Do not use more than 1 oz butter.

Braised Celery

INGREDIENTS:

6 large sticks of celery
1 large diced onion
1 large diced carrot
1 oz butter

½ pt jellied stock
salt and pepper
bouquet garni

DIRECTIONS:

Wash celery, split sticks in two and blanche in boiling salted water and drain. Dice the onion and carrot, sweat them in butter in a pan. Then add the celery, stock, seasoning and bouquet garni. Cover and braise for 1–1½ hours or until tender. Baste well from time to time.

91

Plum Pudding

INGREDIENTS:

½ lb breadcrumbs
½ lb chopped suet
¼ lb flour
½ lb brown sugar
1 tsp spice
½ tsp nutmeg
1 tsp baking powder
¼ lb chopped almonds

¼ lb currants
¼ lb raisins
¼ lb sultanas
¼ lb mixed peel
4 eggs
½ bottle Guinness
rind and juice of 1 lemon
  and 1 orange

DIRECTIONS:

Mix breadcrumbs, suet, sugar and flour together. Add the spices, grated lemon and orange rind, currants, raisins, sultanas, peel and almonds. Mix well and leave overnight if possible. Next day add baking powder, eggs, lemon and orange juice and Guinness. Turn into a greased bowl or floured pudding cloth. Cover bowl with greaseproof paper and then with pudding cloth. If using floured pudding cloth gather it up and tie tightly and put so the second tying is four inches higher up. Put plate in the bottom of the saucepan if using a cloth. Have the water boiling and boil for 4 hours. Store in a dry place. The day required, boil for a further two hours. Serve with brandy butter.

For brandy butter:
½ lb butter
¾ lb sieved icing sugar

4 fl oz brandy

DIRECTIONS:

Cream butter and sugar together. Add the brandy. Put into glass storage container and refrigerate until required.

Irish Coffee

INGREDIENTS:

1 tsp sugar
¼ pt strong black coffee
1 tblsp cream

large measure of Irish whiskey

DIRECTIONS:

Dissolve the sugar in the coffee in a warmed long-stemmed whiskey glass. Add whiskey to within 1 inch of the rim and stir. Hold a teaspoon upside down over the liquid, then gently pour the cream so that it floats on the surface. Do not stir, but drink the coffee through the cold cream.

Mince Pies

INGREDIENTS:

1 lb shortcrust pastry
1½ lb sweet mincemeat

1–2 tblsps brandy or rum or
  sherry
castor sugar for dusting

DIRECTIONS:

On a lightly floured surface, roll out half the pastry fairly thinly and stamp into rounds with a cutter. Put rounds to one side. Add trimmings to second half of the pastry and roll out a little thinner than first half. Stamp in rounds, a little larger than first. Mix brandy, rum or sherry with mincemeat. Put larger pastry rounds into patty tins, with a good spoonful of mincemeat to fill well. Place smaller rounds on top, pinch pastry edges together, brush lightly with cold water and dust with sugar. Cook for 15–20 minutes until nicely brown. Cool slightly before taking from tins.

Christmas Cake

INGREDIENTS:

8 oz plain flour
pinch of salt
½ tsp ground cinnamon
½ grated nutmeg
1 lb sultanas
12 oz seeded raisins
8 oz glacé cherries

4 oz shredded almonds
2 oz chopped candied peel
6 oz butter
grated rind of ½ lemon
6 oz dark brown sugar
4 beaten eggs
2 tblsps brandy

DIRECTIONS:

Prepare cake tin with a double thickness of greaseproof paper. Sift the flour with the salt and spices into a bowl, then divide mixture into three portions. Mix one portion with the prepared fruit, almonds and peel. Beat the butter until soft, add the lemon rind and sugar and continue beating until very soft. Add the eggs one at a time, beating well between each one, then use a metal spoon to fold in a second portion of flour. Mix in the remaining flour, and brandy. Turn the mixture into the prepared tin and smooth the top of the cake. Moisten the surface very slightly with warm water. Put the cake in the middle of the oven and bake for about 2¼ hours. After 1 hour reduce the heat of the oven and cover the top with a double thickness of greaseproof paper. Allow the cake to cool for about 30 minutes in the tin and then turn it on to a rack and leave until cold. Christmas cakes are traditionally iced with almond paste and white icing.